Setting Up & Using Your HSA

© 2023
by Aaron Brachfeld
ISBN: 9798373510950

Though the author of this book is a licensed insurance agent and has decades of experience, and even lectures in the subject, this book does not constitute legal or tax advice and should not be construed as doing so.

There are many reasons to get an HSA, but one reason why people don't is because they are complicated to set up and use.

This book makes it easy and presents all you need to know about how to set up and use an HSA: complicated subjects like how to use an HSA to reduce your tax burden, how to use an HSA as a retirement vehicle, how to avoid tax penalties when using it, how to calculate your share of major medical expenses and what records to keep and how are presented.

The author is a licensed insurance agent in the State of Colorado, with additional State certification in the Insurance Marketplace and decades of experience who teaches on the subject at Western Colorado Community College.

Table of Contents

2 Kinds of HSA's	6
Why Get an HSA? Tax Benefits	8
2 Kinds of HSA Bank Accounts	11
3 Parts of an HSA Insurance Plan	15
What Can You Spend Your HSA Money On?	20
What Happens When You're Older than 65?	22
How Much Can You Contribute to an HSA?	24
What Preventative Care is Included for Free?	26
How to Use the HSA's	29
Record Keeping and Tax Form	32
Where Can You Learn More About HSA's?	34

2 Kinds of HSA's

An HSA stands for "Health Savings Account," and confusingly, HSA may mean one of two different things.

    An HSA is a kind of insurance policy
    An HSA is a kind of Bank Account

Why Get an HSA? Tax Benefits

People get HSA's for two reasons. First, the HSA usually offers the cheapest out of pocket protection per premium dollar: in other words, it offers more affordable major medical emergency protection, and is therefore ideal for people in high risk occupations, or those people who know they will have expensive medical costs in the coming year - such as a birth, or major surgery.

However, not all HSA's offer this superior emergency coverage and you should talk to your insurance agent and ask for help in calculating which plan would best serve your needs.

The other reason is the tax advantage.

When you put money into your HSA bank account, you can reduce your total taxable income - even if you do not itemize your deductions on Schedule A of Form 1040.

And, if your employer makes contributions to your HSA bank account for you, these may be excluded from your gross income.

Contributions made to your HSA bank account remain in there until you use them. And interest (or investment earnings) on these funds are tax free too.

2 Kinds of HSA Bank Accounts

The HSA bank account may be established with a bank, investment firm, or even the insurance company itself - but not all banks, investment firms, or insurance companies offer this kind of account.

Whether you switch insurance companies next year or not, you may keep using your same bank account.

And, whether or not you switch what bank you have your bank account with, you may keep using your same insurance company.

There are two kinds of HSA bank accounts.

Some function just like normal savings accounts, and might be linked with your checking account.

There are also HSA bank accounts that are linked to investment accounts: rather than transferring funds between the savings account and your checking account, these allow you to transfer money between the savings account and an investment account, which can be used to purchase stocks, mutual funds and other investments.

Some people will use their HSA regularly. But others have minimal health expenses during a year, and for them, it makes sense to risk investments that might pay off in the long term more than they might earn in simple interest on a savings account.

And, if the funds grow in that investment account faster than they are able to be used, upon retirement age, these funds may be used in many other ways - functioning as a tax advantaged savings, in many ways similar to an IRA.

We will look at this a little closer later.

3 Parts of an HSA Insurance Plan

The HSA insurance plan has 3 parts.

First, the out of pocket maximum: this is the most you will spend on medical expenses during the coverage year. Any covered medical expenses beyond that, except for copays, will be paid for by the insurance company. Entirely. 100%.

Second, the deductible. You are entirely responsible for medical costs up to the deductible. For many HSA's, this is equal to the out of pocket maximum, meaning after this amount is paid, the insurance company will pay the rest.

Third, coinsurance. Some HSA's have coinsurance. This is the share of medical cost you are responsible for after the deductible, but before the out of pocket maximum.

If your deductible is equal to your out of pocket maximum, you will have a coinsurance of 0%, since the insurance company is paying for everything after that.

If your out of pocket maximum is more than your deductible, and your coinsurance is 20%, you will pay 20% of every dollar until you spend your out of pocket maximum.

For example, let's pretend you are going to have a $15,000 operation.

Plan A

Deductible: $7,000
Out of Pocket Maximum: $7,000
Coinsurance: 0%

Cost of operation = $15,000
Minus the $7,000 deductible = $8,000
You have already spent the $7,000 deductible, so the remaining amount is subject to the coinsurance:
$8,000 x 0% = $0.
Total spent: $7,000 deductible + $0 coinsurance
= $0 total spent

Plan B

Deductible: $7,000
Out of Pocket Maximum: $3,500
Coinsurance: 20%

Cost of operation = $15,000
Minus the $3,500 deductible = 11,500
You have already spent the $3,500 deductible, so the remaining amount is subject to the coinsurance:
$11,500 x 20% = $2,300.
Total spent = $3,500 deductible + $2,300 coinsurance
= **$5,800 total spent**

What Can You Spend Your HSA Money On?

You can use these funds on any qualified medical expense - even if your HSA insurance plan does not cover it. For example, though your health insurance might not cover eye glasses, the dentist or even fertility treatments, or even the costs of hotels and travel out of State to get advanced treatments, you may use money in your HSA bank account to pay for these.

If you use your HSA on non-medical expenses, you will pay income tax on that money, as well as a 20% penalty. Unless you're older than 65.

Check out IRS Publication 502 for a full list of what is considered "Medical" expenses.

What Happens When You're Older than 65?

When you reach retirement age, these funds may be used for many non-medical expenses as well. However, if used on non-medical expenses, they may be subject to taxation as income - but without the 20% penalty.

This is why many retirees will use their HSA's to pay for medical expenses even into retirement: premiums for medicare parts A, B, and D do count as medical expenses. If these are automatically withdrawn from your social security check, you can refund yourself out of your HSA tax free.

How Much Can You Contribute to an HSA?

The amount you can contribute to the HSA bank account with this tax advantage changes every year, but has historically been over $3,600 for an individual covered by an HSA insurance plan, and $7,200 for a family covered by an HSA insurance plan. And these figures usually increase every year.

You can make these contributions at any time during the year, from January through December, but if you miss this opportunity, you can usually make a contribution to the account as late as April the year following.

What Preventative Care is Included for Free?

Preventative care is almost always included for free in the HSA Insurance coverage. Preventative care may include:

Periodic health evaluations, including tests and diagnostic procedures ordered in connection with routine examinations, such as annual physicals.

Routine prenatal and well-child care.

Child and adult immunizations.

Tobacco cessation programs.

Obesity weight-loss programs.

Screening services. This includes screening services for

- Cancer
- Heart and vascular diseases
- Infectious diseases

Mental health conditions
Substance abuse.
Metabolic, nutritional, and endocrine conditions
Musculoskeletal disorders.
Obstetric and gynecological conditions
Pediatric conditions
Vision and hearing disorders

How to Use the HSA's

If you have already deposited money into your HSA bank account, it is an easy thing to simply use your HSA debit card or checks to pay for medical expenses that come up.

But if you haven't, when you see the doctor, or go to the Urgent Care or Emergency Room, many banks will let you quickly and easily move money into your HSA from your checking account into your HSA bank account for free on the same day with a "bank transfer."

Many people will transfer only the amount that is due for the medical expense that day, and then instantly spend it: their HSA bank account is a "pass through" account, where money is not kept for savings, but immediately spent.

However, some medical expenses are so large that they have to be spread over many years. If you were covered by an HSA insurance plan at the time the medical expense was incurred, and maintain that HSA insurance plan, you may contribute funds to your HSA bank account every year, and use those funds to pay the medical payment plan over time, spreading out the cost and the tax benefit.

Record Keeping and Tax Form

You will want to keep records, such as bills and receipts, showing that money coming from your HSA account were used exclusively to pay for medical expenses, and that those medical expenses were not taken as an itemized deduction in any year. You don't send these records in with your tax return, but keep them in case the IRS may ask for them in the future.

If you use your HSA for non-medical expenses you could face a 20% penalty on those funds.

When you want to claim the tax deduction for using your HSA, you will use Form 8889 from the IRS.

Where Can You Learn More About HSA's?

IRS Publication 969 has much more detailed information about HSA's.

You will also want to contact an insurance agent. Most agents will not charge you for consultation or to explain things. However, they may ask you to designate them as your agent, so they may legally comply with HIPAA.

www.ingramcontent.com/pod-product-compliance
Lightning Source LLC
Chambersburg PA
CBHW050325220526
45465CB00005B/2140